About the author

Graham Andrews is a professional writer living on the South Coast of New South Wales. He has worked as a scientific editor, technical writer, freelance writer and writing tutor.

By the same author

A Guide to Wrought Iron and Welding

You're On Air

Easy Guide to Creative Writing

In Your New Image

Easy Guide to Science and Technical Writing

Island of the Barking Dog

Dad Kept Bees

Reach For the Sky

Practical Arc Welding

Easy Guide to
Writing Winning Essays

A guide to writing essays
for university or college

Graham J Andrews

Flairnet

First published 2014
Copyright © 2014 Graham J Andrews

ISBN 978-0-9924642-3-3

Published by Flairnet
www.flairnet.com.au
Post Office 645
Narooma NSW 2546
Australia

National Library of Australia Cataloguing-in-Publication entry

Author: Andrews, Graham J., author.

Title: Easy guide to writing winning essays : a guide to writing essays for university or college / Graham J Andrews.

ISBN: 9780992464233 (paperback)

Notes: Includes index.

Subjects: Essay--Technique.
Academic writing.
English language--Rhetoric.

Dewey Number: 808.4

Contact the author:
Website: www.grahamandrews.com
Email: graham@grahamandrews.com

Contents

Introduction

How many students dread the day they have to hand in their essays? Possibly most of them. Students delay that day until the very last minute, because the task ahead of them seems so daunting. And the task seems so daunting because most students are ill-prepared to write 2000 words or 3000 words on a topic selected not by them, but by their professor or their teacher.

The result is usually a hurried affair, showing poor structure, poor grammar, resulting in poor marks.

And yet the task of writing a good essay is no more involved than the task of writing a bad essay—probably about an extra hour's work at the most would be involved. And that hour could result in perhaps many more marks.

It's not just good luck that some students appear gifted when it comes to the task of writing winning essays. The difference lies in their preparation, and the time students spend planning their assignments each

7

time, and in the time they devote to constructing the essay in a sensible, logical way, showing steady progression of ideas, so the subject evolves.

The task of writing good essays is not beyond the average student. Provided, that is, the student wants to achieve good marks for his or her effort, and provided the student is prepared to learn.

I have lost count of the students who have enrolled in my Writing Winning Essays course and have not even bothered to take note of the points I have made for their benefit. They repeat the same mistakes over and over in each subsequent essay. Is it any wonder that these students never seem to get marks above a very meagre 'pass' grade?

Yet others are keen to learn—indeed, most are very keen to learn from their mistakes. After all, if they learn something from writing one essay, the task of writing the next essay is so much easier.

The idea of your teacher or professor getting you to write essays has more than one purpose. It's to help develop your research methods. It's to help you think logically—and all good essays should be thought out logically. But the reason is also to help you develop

Introduction

writing skills that are of a very high level, skills that will equip you well when you have finished your course and join the workforce.

And if you can write well during the early years of your career, then you can expect to be, or rather should be, rewarded for your skills with higher salary and faster promotion.

And if you do develop those writing skills that are so essential in your career, there's a very good chance you will stand out from the others in your office, laboratory or department.

Your teacher or professor will notice your efforts at writing winning essays. Your supervisor in later life will admire you for these same skills. Now is the time to learn how to write winning essays!

Chapter 1 What's It About?

This little book will help you work your way successfully through the essays that form an important part of many of your subjects in your chosen course.

Writing essays is an important part of any university or college qualification. A large portion of term or semester marks are awarded for the way you, the student, write essays. A good essay means good marks, higher grades, and so on. You get the message!

This book will help you prepare winning essays that will earn you excellent marks. I won't be writing the essays for you, but I will show you how to write an essay that will reward you for your efforts.

The good news is that writing a good essay is not much harder than writing a bad one. Only the marks you would get for each type would be different.

Having got to your present level of studies, I assume you have a reasonable command of the English language. I can't teach you grammar and make you a good speller. But through this book I can work with the skills you have and teach you how to develop your essay-writing talents.

The level of skills you attain after reading this book is partly up to how you apply what I have shown you. But I do expect your marks will improve significantly, based on my past experience at helping other students learn the art of good essay writing.

Essay writing is, really, quite easy. As I mentioned, it is not much harder to write a good essay than it is to write a bad one.

Unlike with conversation where we have the benefit of hand movements, facial expressions and posture to get our message across to a listener, an essay must be clear in the words that we write. And unlike a conversation where we can repeat something we have just said—several times, and at a simpler level if necessary—with essays, no such privilege is permitted.

Unlike with conversational English, where the speaker can cover a dozen topics in a dozen sentences, rapidly changing from one subject to the next, an essay must be clear, concise, well ordered and logical in its flow and treatment from the start.

You will delete all repetition. You will delete all clichés—those useless, worn-out phrases that mean little. And delete any word that doesn't add anything to the work. And then see if you can delete even further. In other words, there will be no repetition, no padding out the paragraphs or pages hoping your lecturer or tutor won't know what you are trying to do. The result will be good, clear, clean copy that says ... well, exactly what you were asked to say.

Unlike other writing we may be engaged in, like writing for a newspaper or a newsletter, where we will have an interest in what we are telling the readers, many essays are about subjects we might know very little about. After all, that's one of the reasons why the topics are set—so you, the student, can acquire the skills necessary to research the material, come up with all the facts that are pertinent to your point of view, and then put them in a clear, logical order. And hopefully learn about another topic in the process.

You might (like just about every other student who has ever attended university or college) consider essays as complete @#*&$! At first you're probably right. But they serve a worthwhile purpose, believe it or not. They teach you analytical skills. They teach you writing skills. And they teach you how to express yourself clearly. And they're important to train you in research methods. All of these are things you will need to use after you graduate or go on to do higher study.

Having got a job using your degree or diploma, you will be expected to write discussion papers or persuasive arguments to put up to committees who will want something clear to discuss. The committee members will want facts, not waffle. The skills you acquire in learning to write essays will be more valuable than you might realise right now.

Even ten years after graduation, you will need to know how to look up relevant facts in the library, know what is good value and what is written trash. You will need to know what you can rely on and particularly what you cannot rely on at all for your source material. I don't like to take the side of your professors or your teachers, but just this once, they do, I hate to admit, know what they are doing.

Here are some points that will help you.

What's It About?

You can learn to write good essays. Please believe it.

You can remove the procrastination and write them early in the semester, not the night before you are due to present them. That, too, is true. I'm a journalist—would I lie to you?

You can always get enough material to write about. Everything you need to know is there, in your library. As I said, I'm a journalist ...

And you can learn to present your essay so it is neat, tidy, and shows the required level of professionalism your lecturer would expect from you. You are, after all, at quite a high level in your education, so make the most of what you have achieved so far.

Chapter 2 Important Considerations

You must consider your readership. Who is your readership when you write your essay? Of course, it's your teacher, or your professor. Write it for them. Write it at perhaps a higher level than you would if you were writing an article for a popular magazine or a newspaper. But that does not mean that the language has to be so complicated that only your professor would understand your work. No, keep it simple, but keep it intelligent.

TYPE FACE

Some type faces (or fonts) are easier to read than others, especially if your teacher has to read 90,000 words (30 essays, by 3000 words each). The fonts that are easiest to read are those with serifs—the little feet—such as Times Roman (but use at least 12 point for Times Roman as it is a very small newspaper font), or New Century.

Important Considerations

Fancy fonts are painful on the eyes. Think of your reader—your teacher!

GETTING STARTED

This first point is not about writing, but about psychology. It is called motivating yourself. It could also be called stop procrastinating. Or making a start. Often that first sentence is the hardest of all to write. Once that is written, the next might flow slightly more easily. And the third might be even easier.

But back to that first sentence.

After you have completed your research for the assignment, you might find this is a way of getting the words to start flowing. If they don't come to you straight away, start writing or typing anything—gibberish, a joke or two, just anything to get the words flowing. If the words that come to you relate to your assignment, so much the better. If not, write a few sentences, but don't go over one page. If nothing meaningful has come to your mind in that time, leave it and concentrate on it another time.

If you follow these simple instructions, then, believe it or not, the rest of the task is much, much more straight forward!

But that's enough psychology. You certainly don't want to be told to work with a tidy desk, or to clean up your room to put you in a better frame of mind, or skip that extra cup of coffee, turn off the television or radio, don't call your friends or telephone that special someone.

WHAT IS THE QUESTION?

It might sound simple, but it is surprising just how many students get poor marks, not through their lack of writing ability, but because they have not read the question properly, or have not understood it. Read it, get a picture of what you are required to write about, and make sure that you really have understood what is required of you. Some academics are terrible at expressing themselves. So if you think the question could have two meanings, or there is something not clear to you, then clarify what is meant, and what you are meant to write about. It's easier to correct the direction of your work at this early stage than end up writing the wrong essay.

Important Considerations

No matter how well you have written your assignment, if it does not answer the question fully, then don't expect top marks. Marks are, in addition to a lot of other things, awarded for the relevance of what you write to what you were asked to write.

There are usually few words in the question, but some of them are critical to your success or otherwise. Such words are **discuss**: this means just that—discuss it!

Another word is **compare**. That means take two, three maybe, points of view, and contrast or compare one with the other, or others. Show which of those views has more merit, which argument is more valid. Which argument has no substance. That's what's wanted when you are asked to compare some topic.

Explain is another word that creeps into essay questions.

Another one is **contrast**. Contrast is a little like compare, except that the points of view you are discussing are usually opposites.

Some of your examiners might try to seem difficult. They will ask you to compare and contrast different points of view. Actually, they are not trying to be difficult. They merely want you to look at similarities and differences between the points of view under consideration, that's all.

So if you are asked to explain something, don't compare two points of view. If you are asked to contrast two views, don't explain only one in detail.

Many students find it a great help if they use a highlighting pen to make such words stand out. There can be no mistaking in their minds exactly what is required of them. Try doing the same yourself.

But let's look again at those, and other, definitions.

Compare. This means write about both sides of an argument, or look at both the similarities and the differences to a topic.

Contrast. This means there are usually two points of view, and you are required to look at both of them.

Define. This means giving the exact meaning and expanding on it.

Discuss. Here, you would need to look at all aspects (remember there could well be more than two points of view) and debate them. Generally you would give reasons and arguments for and against each point.

Evaluate. You would be required to consider the merits of some point of view, and discuss its value, its relevance, its accuracy or whatever.

Illustrate. You would use examples to prove or to substantiate your points.

Outline. Write about the general features or at least the main points of the topic (or aspect of the subject), but you would concentrate on the main elements of the viewpoint.

But with many questions, you will find there is no clear-cut answer. You might find overwhelming evidence for one view, and little to support the opposing view (especially ideas expressed by notable authorities on the subject). At other times, there might not be a clear answer one way or the other. In any case, perhaps any of these treatments might be valid. If you need to sit on the fence, undecided, then sit there and look equally at both sides of the argument. Don't feel you necessarily have to fall off the pickets in either direction.

If you find you can put in extreme viewpoints, then put them in, but only if there is published material to support your way of thinking.

TAKING THE HARD OPTION

Often you will be given a choice of questions. This does not always make your job easier, especially if you're not really interested in any of them. But often you will find that what at first seems to be the hardest question of all is the easiest one to answer. Not always, but it's worth considering.

Chapter 3 Researching Your Topic

Research and reference material is essential if you are going to write any good essay.

Always base your arguments and points of view on published material. While it is easy to say, in effect, 'this is what I think about it ...' unfortunately this is not the way essays are prepared. It's a funny thing about writing essays. If you write an article for a magazine or a newspaper, even a popular magazine, you, as author, can be quoted (even by students writing essays). If, however, you write the same words in an essay without substantiating the facts from published works, then expect lower marks. Look on the bright side. When you get published, either during your course or after graduating, then you can seek revenge on other students.

One place that has numerous points that you will find interesting is an index of a book on the subject. Scan the index just for joggers—those points that jump out at you and you can say—Eureka, that's one. Eureka, there's another, and so on.

You can research your essay using a wide range of reference material. But, like many things in life, there are good sources and many not-so-good sources. And, there are the terrible ones.

Books and journals are usually refereed. This means that any article that is received by the editor of a journal will be assessed. If it passes the first stage—relevance to the journal, reasonably well written, it seems okay and so on, the editor will send it out to one, usually two and occasionally three people who are experts in that field. The reviewers will comment on the content, pick up (hopefully) all the errors and shortcomings in the article, make other suggestions as to how it can be improved, and send a report back to the editor. If there are serious flaws in the article, then the journal will reject it. Any researcher can be reasonably confident that such an article published in a journal will be factual, and thus reliable.

The same applies to most books other than novels and the like. But popular magazines? The referee system is not usually used, and many magazines adopt the 'anything goes in if it looks about right' attitude.

As for newspapers, I don't think they have a policy on accuracy at all (well, many of them don't, anyway). So don't quote from them unless there's no alternative, or if your essay question is 'Do you think newspapers are a reliable source of research information for students writing essays? Please discuss this statement'.

When using journal articles and books as your source of information, don't make your essay a series of direct quotes. That would look as if you are unable to interpret what others have written. A poor mark can be guaranteed. Interpret the information, and write about it in your own way, in your style, but give credit to the author whose work you have used by means of listing and identifying references (more on that later).

Your research is going to provide you with all the source material that you will need. Take a hint. When you note down a fact, write down its source also. It is extremely (and I don't like using superlatives too often) frustrating to have that gem of a quote, find that you might have misquoted it slightly, and forgotten where you got it from. Write down its source, as in the book or journal, its page number, and its library catalogue number. Many a student has used such a gem, the teacher has queried its accuracy, and the student has failed to find it again and regain an extra mark or two.

You will need the title of the journal, the title of the article you referred to, its author or authors (all of them), the date and, if a book, the publisher, for your reference list.

When researching your topic, take lots of notes. If your writing is neat and tidy, that's fine. If it looks like spider crawlings, type your notes.

If there is so much material available on your topic, you might think you are lucky. But the problem you will face is sorting it all out, sifting out only what you need, and not to get sidetracked by finding references that take you in a direction that is different from what the question asked for. But you might face the opposite difficulty too, and find insufficient material to compile anything like the 3000 words you were asked for. Believe it or not, there really is sufficient material in your library for your assignment. Or there might be plenty of material in another library that your education establishment has access to. Some teachers and professors try to see how ingenious their students are by setting questions where reference material is limited in the institute's library, but where there is a profusion of good reference material in the library of another institution. You might (but no guarantees here) get a slightly better mark for showing initiative and going to another library, just to show your teacher that you can outwit him. I know that works sometimes, but I cannot guarantee anything with your teacher!

Remember that it is not only the 3000 words your teacher wants—it is high quality 3000 words. Almost anyone can write 3000 words, only a skilled person can put quality in that quantity of work.

Chapter 4 Starting to Write

When do you start the writing itself? That's simple. Only when you have gathered all your reference material. That way, you can sort out (at least, in your mind) what is there, what else you might need, work out how you are going to approach the subject, and what you are going to do with that material you have (that is, what angle will you take, what tone will you use, what style will you use).

Let us say that you have been busy in your library, have gathered all the reference material that you will need to do justice to the subject you are writing about, and are ready to begin. Don't just start writing. You will need a plan. This is nothing more than an idea of what you are going to cover, points of view, and the order in which you will address those relevant points.

Many students find the writing task so much easier to perform (and complete) if they break down their work into small, manageable segments, like building bricks.

You can work with bricks of a size you know you can handle. They might be small, such as three sentences. Your bricks might be single paragraphs. You know you can write a paragraph. You have done it before.

And, just like it is in real life when building a house with bricks, one brick is added to the previous one, essay writing using bricks (or, more correctly, paragraphs) is not much different. One paragraph is added to the previous one, the next is added to that, and so on.

Soon (after maybe six or ten paragraphs) you will have one page. And then you will add one writing brick at the start of the next page, and add the next writing brick to that one and so on until you have constructed a second page. And the second page is added to the first, and so on. In other words, a house is built brick by brick. An essay is built paragraph by paragraph.

DETERMINE THE SIZE OF YOUR BRICKS

What size chunks can you work with, and how many of them will you need?

Let's say you can work with paragraphs of six or seven sentences, each with about fifteen words. That's a convenient, easy size to work with.

Let's assume your essay is required to be 3000 words—the average length for second and final year university assignments. That means you will need about 30 bricks, or paragraphs, each around 100 words.

Break down you assignment into those 30 or so bricks, by the use of headings. It's like writing only one hundred words about a topic. Anyone can do that! And then, for the next heading, you write another hundred words. Anyone can do that too!

So create as many headings as you can (and include many of those points you gleaned from scanning the indexes of relevant books too).

Let's say you were asked to discuss the availability of primary health care to marginalised groups—the unemployed, single parent families, Indigenous groups, those from ethnic and culturally diverse backgrounds (a government term for migrants), the homeless, youth and anyone else who might see themselves disadvantaged for the occasion.

Some of the headings that come to mind immediately might include: an introduction, what the problem is, the place of the individual in the socio-economic bracket, what are inequalities as far as the delivery of primary health services, what is the correlation between being disadvantaged and poor health, is the problem universal, or does it apply only in your country, life expectancies, longevity, how socio-economic status affects health—the influence of the pecking order in society—poor housing, poor water supplies, lack of opportunities for immunisation, ineffective education and health promotion campaigns. Education is important here, and so is isolation. Consider too whether the message of immunisation and exercise programs to promote good health is too difficult to get across to these people, and so on until you have found your mandatory thirty headings.

The next thing to do is to rearrange each and every one of those possible headings in a sensible, logical order. If several of them jump out, you might be able to use these as main headings, and sort the others below them, as appropriate, as sub-headings. That way, all similar arguments will be together, and you will be able to move from one point to the next. Try to get similar numbers of sub-headings under each of your main headings—but don't do the impossible if you can't.

It's often a good idea to arrange such headings along the lines of: what the problem is, the evidence for it, what is the cause of the problem.

Then the second part of your essay could cover what can reasonably be done to help such people. There will be ways that general practitioners can at least be seen to be doing something—providing clinics operating in remote districts part-time, promoting education programs of their own on a regional basis, becoming acquainted with the customs and beliefs of Indigenous and migrant groups. There would of course be a few et ceteras thrown in here too.

The third part of your essay could be controversial if you are permitted to do this, so check your teacher's or professor's sense of humour first.

Again, even this controversial part will need to be well ordered, with the arguments for doing little and achieving little in providing primary health care being written—need I say it again—in a logical, well-reasoned order.

So now you have read the essay question, and you actually understand it. This puts you ahead of a lot of the students! You're off to a good start. You've even got all the headings, arranged them into the correct order, you have done your research, and you are ready to begin. But one word of caution. Unless you are asked to do otherwise, if you put forward both sides of any argument, give each point of view about equal space. To give one side of an argument several times more words than you allocate to the opposite view clearly indicates your bias—and you're not supposed to have any bias! Strive for that goal later!

First, you will need an introduction to the essay. This is usually no more than two or three paragraphs about the subject—perhaps a very broad overview—or as some would call it, a global picture of the topic. That's like a broad, sweeping view in a few short sentences. Then, you get into the real essay.

To begin writing, I suggest to students that they keep the first heading at the top of the computer screen, and the second heading about six or eight lines below it. That way, the next heading will be visible and you will be aware of what the next part of the essay will be about. As for the rest of the headings, put in a page break and push the whole lot of them over to the next page out of sight. There will be only two headings on the page you are writing on: the heading of the section you are currently writing, and the next heading only.

As you finish the first treatment and begin on the second, bring up the next heading and keep that about six or eight lines below the section you are working on. Forget about the others for now by leaving them all on the next page.

Before you know it, you will have written about a hundred words against each of those topics you listed as headings, and there you are. At least, for the time being.

THE CONCLUSION

You will need to make some conclusions. If you are stuck on that fence, then say why you can't get off the palings. Say that no point of view is defined clearly enough in any of the material you have researched. But usually in your conclusion (which only needs to be two or three paragraphs long) you will need to explain why you think this way, why you reject that view, why someone hasn't been able to come up with the right answers either. No firm view can be quite a valid viewpoint in its own right.

OVERWRITING

I tend to overwrite. That means, if I need to write an article of say 2000 words, then I aim for around 2500 words. The reason is simple. If I need 2000 words and I have only 2000 words, then I am going to be reluctant to throw any of them away. If I have 500 words I don't need, then I have plenty of room to pick and choose. And since there is truth in the old saying that writing improves in direct proportion to the number of words thrown out, then by throwing out twenty percent, the work's just got to improve markedly. So, overwrite, and throw out all unnecessary words. It might seem like unnecessary energy, but you will come to appreciate the wisdom of this attitude.

Chapter 5 Editing

You've written the first draft, now it's time to edit the result. This is the same as tidying up your essay. Clean up what you have written. Make sure that each sentence says only one thing. If not, break it down into two or more sentences. Make sure that each paragraph stands alone—that is, each sentence really does belong in that paragraph and that each paragraph looks at only one thing.

And do the same with headings—make sure that each paragraph you have written really belongs under the right heading. If it doesn't, cut and paste it into the right place.

Remember, the first draft is just that—a rough, first attempt at putting all your thoughts down on the subject. That attempt might seem a little rough, but there's nothing wrong with having what might seem a disaster of words of a high magnitude—as long as you can do something with those words to breathe life into the essay, tidy up the work, clean up the text, make sure every sentence, every paragraph is just right. Unless your first draft is excellent (if it was, you would not be reading this book on essay writing), you will need to revise your essay perhaps several times and check through it again and again until you can't find anything wrong with it. And then it is ready to hand in to your teacher or professor.

But there are a few things you need to watch out for.

Use short words, not long words.

Remove all adjectives and adverbs, such as very, extremely, so many, unless you have to use them.

When you are writing and editing your work, try to put in linking phrases between paragraphs so each does not stand out as if it is built on stilts. Remember, your essay is one work, not a series of short pieces that are distinct from each other. Use blending phrases that imply ' ... which leads me to say ... ', 'however ...', 'on the other hand, ...' and so on. Such little phrases will make your whole work seem less disjointed, more as one paper, and more enjoyable to read.

During each edit, you will need to check the sentences, making sure they are of an appropriate length (about fifteen words on average is a good length to be aiming for). Make sure the paragraphs do not go on for one whole page. About six or seven sentences each would be fine.

Make sure the language and style you have used are suitable. Take out all clichés—they're those old, clapped out phrases like 'putting something on the back burner', 'level playing field', 'buttering your bread', or 'knowing on which side it's buttered', 'window of opportunity'. They're useless, and don't really say much. Often they are used so inappropriately that they become humorous. Think of something original. Be yourself (within reason).

Don't use colloquial expressions either—such as he booted the ball, the satellite was rocketed into orbit. Yuck!

And in your edits, make sure about your grammar. Make sure the possessives really are that and your teacher knows who owns what—'the professor's chair ...' Check a good grammar book if you are in any doubt.

Check also that a single noun has a single verb, and that a plural noun goes with a plural verb. Don't write 'he or she are ...', or 'his practitioners believes that ...' and so on.

At the final stage, you can make sure that the presentation is exactly as it should be. If your teacher prefers double spacing, give him double spacing. If he prefers wide margins so he can write sarcastic comments, give him plenty of room for his pleasure. You may prefer to use single spacing while you are writing it—this certainly is easier, as you have more text in front of you to work with, and because the lines are much easier to see.

Editing is your chance to:

- Ensure a logical progression of ideas, rearrange the sequence of topic headings, paragraphs and sentences;

- Expand or reduce text to improve the quality of the essay, to remove inappropriate words, vagueness;

- Break up long sentences or paragraphs so the text is easier to follow;

- Check that the headings and sub-headings are still appropriate to what follows them;

- Check again the required word limit and the length of your essay;

- Improve the quality of the essay so it is of literary brilliance!

Always remember that if in the editing you make changes to the text, ensure that appropriate changes are made to the abstract (if you have one).

Don't keep the essay at its original length merely to make it appear a long composition. Remember that saying that all writing improves in proportion to the amount of words left out. Once you have completed the first edit (which should be a heavy edit, eliminating all possible words you don't need), go through again and eliminate more that you don't need. Do this until you get to the stage where it is impossible to delete even one more word. And then it should be all right!

Other points to watch for in your editing include:

- Don't join a number of sentences together with 'and';

- Use simple words rather than complex words — words of two syllables rather than five syllables;

- Avoid unnecessary words;

- An attitude of indifference — you must consider your teacher's or professor's background;

- Remove vague, meaningless and wrong words — replace these with concise words and phrases;

Editing

- Jargon—replace with simple, precise terms or clearly defined terms;

- Remove wordiness—remove all redundancies;

- Remove tautologies, clichés; and

- Convert the passive voice to the active voice where possible.

Chapter 6 References

References can be painful. They needn't be, though. In the real world (that is, after your graduation), references are included in many articles merely to show readers where the information you have quoted came from so they can read more about the subject for themselves if they are interested. By including references in your essay, you will be getting valuable experience in using references correctly, and in compiling reference lists for those papers you will probably write once you become part of the real world. So it's important to learn about references while you have the chance, so now is a good time to learn about them.

There are two systems of referencing used. The first is the Harvard system. In the text, when referring to a passage written by an author, simply put in brackets the name and year of that author (Bloggs, 1992) and then you will need to make sure that you list his work in the reference section at the end of your paper. If two authors said much the same thing (Bloggs, 1992; Nurks, 1997) then separate the two using a semi colon. Make sure both references are included in your reference list.

In the reference list, all references will appear in alphabetical order. If there are two or three by an author of the same name, they should be listed in date order. If two by the same author were published in the same year, separate them by making them a and b (Bloggs 1997a; Bloggs 1997b).

If there are numerous authors for an article you are quoting, you need only include the first couple, followed by *et al.*

The second system of referencing is the Vancouver system. This is used mainly for medical texts, and can drive a writer mad, and an editor insane (if you send papers later on to a journal). Why? Because they are listed by means of a number (actually, a superscript) in the order in which they are used in the text. So if you decide you need to add another reference in paragraph one, then you will need to change all the references throughout the paper or essay, and the reference list too.

Also, the titles of journals and books are treated differently to the Harvard system.

REFERENCE LIST

A list of references forms an important part of your essay. It gives credit to the authors whose works you have used.

Let's look at the Harvard system first. As mentioned, these references are listed in alphabetical order. If it's a journal article, you will need the author and his initials, the title of the journal, its volume and issue number. And get the titles right.

If a book, then you will need to quote the author, or authors, the title of the book and its publisher and place of publication.

For the Harvard referencing system, as a general rule, the author's name goes first, then his initials, then the date. If a journal article, this goes in apostrophes (' ... ') and the name of the journal goes in italics. If you are quoting a book, then the title of the book goes in italics.

Here are some examples.

Bloggs, G.J. 1998(a), 'Writing essays—the definitive student guide', *University Results* 67; 3-6.

References

Bloggs, G.J. 1998(b), 'Why students fail', *Curriculum* 64;
9-12.

Nurks, A.S. 1991, *Every Student's Guide to Essay
Writing*, Doghouse Publishing, New York.

Now for the Vancouver system. As mentioned earlier, this is used mainly for medical referencing.

The order of things is different, and nothing at all goes in italics. Under this system, each reference will be numbered according to the order in which it was cited in your essay. Nothing could be simpler, could it?

1. Bloggs GJ, Nurks BL, Writing medical essays—the definitive student guide to passing medical school, University Results 1998:56(6); 44-46.

2. Bloggs GJ, Why students fail, Medical Curriculum 1998:21(1); 3-7.

3. Nurks AS, Every Student's Guide to Essay Writing, New York, Doghouse Publishing 1991.

BIBLIOGRAPHIES

A bibliography is similar to a reference list. Sometimes these can be used as sources for 'further reading' or 'recommended reading'. They are important if you have got ideas from these sources, but have not used the material directly. But treat them the same as references for now.

Chapter 7 Tidying It Up

The beginning of the essay is at the end. Does that make sense?

There are two more pages you will need to complete when you have finished the essay, but they will go at the beginning of the assignment.

The first is the cover sheet—on this you will write the essay topic, the subject you are enrolled in, your teacher, and the question.

The next page can only be written after you have finished the essay. This is the contents page if you require one, but many teachers won't insist on this though. List the main headings, and indent the sub-headings, and include the page numbers.

ABSTRACTS

Sometimes you will need to write an abstract of your essay. An abstract is merely a summary of your work in only one paragraph (although this is usually no way to write a typical paragraph). But one paragraph, about 200 words as a summary of the whole essay is all you will need, if you need one at all. With journal articles, it is often the abstract that gets referenced, so your teacher might get you into the practice of writing them.

Chapter 8 The Final Check

In the final edit, it is essential to check your references. As you go through the text, check that each publication and author is included in your list of references. Be particular about the order of the names of the authors and the year of publication. These are common errors. For example, the reference might be Bloggs and Nerd 1997. In the references, you might refer to Nerds and Bloggs 1996.

In the editing, check for correct abbreviations, and units of measurement.

YOUR CHECKLIST

This is your last chance to get your essay right, and to ensure you get good marks for that essay you have just spent many hours writing. So before submitting your essay, go through the final checklist.

• Does the essay still fall within the scope of the question?

- Does the abstract (if you wrote one) summarise the essay? Is it effective?

- Have I included the title page?

- Have I included the contents page (headings and sub-headings)?

- Is the essay technically sound (no glaring mistakes, nor mistakes of fact)?

- Is the literature review extensive enough? Please use more than one reference.

- Is the conclusion the logical one to draw, or have I missed something?

- Does the literature really mean something I haven't mentioned?

- Have I written the essay well—free from ambiguities, poor sentence construction, punctuation, spelling?

Here is a list of common errors that creep into essay writing:

- Exaggeration of facts;

- Misinterpretation of data, often arising from omission of facts;

- Failure to distinguish between fact and fiction;

- Inconsistencies and contradictions;

- Omission of important topics;

- Incorrect order of sections or paragraphs;

- Incomplete development of a topic;

- Weak beginnings to sections;

- Inclusion of irrelevant, trivial or tedious detail;

- Style that is hard to read;

- Inadequate emphasis on interpretation and conclusions;

- Not clear where the essay is going, and why.

DON'T MAKE EXCUSES

After all this advice has been ignored, and your assignment is very late, remember, you are unlikely to come up with an original excuse. Your teacher or professor has heard them all. Probably many times. Most computers are very reliable—except those being used for writing essays, apparently. The disk failed, the memory chip blew up, the hard disk stopped rotating, there was a three-day power failure, the printer wouldn't respond to the computer, the printer was out of ink or toner or ribbon, the dog chewed up the essay you left at the top of your briefcase, the cat got sick over your work, you didn't have time (not very original), you haven't got around to starting on your essay yet (very common) and many others. Unfortunately, not many of these are original. If you do come up with an original and genuine excuse, you might not get marks deducted for lateness. But don't count on it!

Good luck for now ... And good marks!

Index

Index

CPSIA information can be obtained
at www.ICGtesting.com
Printed in the USA
LVOW08s1458080817

544259LV00013B/818/P